eternity
& oranges

pitt poetry series
ed ochester, editor

eternity
& oranges

Christopher Bakken

Published by the University of Pittsburgh Press, Pittsburgh, Pa., 15260

Copyright © 2016, Christopher Bakken

All rights reserved

Manufactured in the United States of America

Printed on acid-free paper

10 9 8 7 6 5 4 3 2 1

ISBN 13: 978-0-8229-6404-9

ISBN 10: 0-8229-6404-X

for George Kaltsas,
who knows how to swim

Contents

I advise all those who know how to swim never to attempt
to commit suicide by means of the sea. All last night for ten
hours the waves battered me. I drank untold amounts of water,
but every so often without my understanding how, my mouth
came up to the surface. Definitely, sometime when the
opportunity presents itself to me, I'll write my impressions of
a drowning man.

~ **Kostas Karyotakis, suicide note, July 1928** ~

eternity
& oranges

Aubade

We'd not slept in days, or else we were
still sleeping—who could tell?
Few words passed between us then,
yet somehow we heard what the other said.

In that room, we had a copper pot,
a guitar, and a tower of old newspapers.
Fruit you'd cut, now brown on a plate.

From some black clay, you were shaping
a small, tall building with no windows.
It leaned uncomfortably to the left,
as if pressed by hard wind.
You didn't bother to right it.

It had been a long time, one of us
might have said, since the last trucks
returned from the border.

I showed you an ancient silver coin:
on one side, a Gorgon's head,
off-center and missing an ear.

What's this on the other side? I asked.
(I didn't have to ask this aloud).
A stag, maybe, or a bull. We didn't know.
The body was worn away,
but the horns were still sharp.

Just before dawn, some noise
of cats and garbage in the street.
You said, Come with me,
and at last we put down our glasses,
walked in silence to the water,
where one boat was unloading its nets.

First light, fish shining on the dock
like a pile of just-polished knives.

Interior with a Closed Notebook

No doubt you believe you could open it,
pronounce some words at least, but there isn't
any language you recognize, no title
to help you, no annoying epigraph.
Only color offers its clue: the cover is black
and the binding's tight, spiraled like a helix.
No doubt you think your name is written there.

The desk itself is littered with letters,
each stamp demolished by a tire tread
of fading ink. In one of the open books
a whale, or a war, swallows someone whole.
Measure the circumference of the ring
left by the coffee cup. Inspect the veneer
for any imprint the pen forced through the paper.

Beyond the desk, take in the room, the curtains,
the obsolete globe and mangled recliner.
The fireplace is a surprise—its pyramid of ash.
Remember how the little house itself
is troubled by those three quiet dictionaries,
by the headlines you fed up its chimney,
all the lies you'll believe since you have to.

Impressions of a Drowning Man

The night he went down to drown himself
he saw two light bulbs had fizzled
    above the entrance to the café
where just last Saturday he'd dined alone,
    absorbed in his book, smoking a whole pack.

As for his clothes: those he left neatly piled
beneath a riot of oleander,
    folding his jacket to a rectangle,
taking a moment to roll up his tie
    and wedge it inside his vacant left shoe.

It seemed to be inviting him to swim,
the sea. Its exhausted philosophy
    (in suspect collusion with the earth's)
left no room for ordinary human
    distress: it believed so much in itself.

By then the breeze was picking up and waves
were sounding their devotions on the rocks.
    Yes, the fishing boats nodded, *yes*.
From just over the hills, he made out
    the whine of the eight train leaving station.

But nothing like this goes off without a hitch,
even if coins already decorate
    his eyes, and I know he's prepaid the fare.
To imagine him here does not absolve
    me of the meaning of the act. Give them

permission to die, the suicides,
since they owned their lives and chose an ending.
　　　To see them in the fogged-up mirror
of my own worst self does not begin
　　　　　to break earth for the wells they dug themselves.

　　　At bottom, I wouldn't recognize
my own reflection, nor in the haloed
　　　　　porthole peering back upon the sky.
The book of this disaster was scribbled
　　　　　by an interrupting cloud, and shadows

　　　I cast peering down. But he's gone too deep
and I can see how this one's going to fail
　　　　　by succeeding, know that by tomorrow
he'll find another way to finish it.
　　　　　So it's safe to watch him wading, permit

　　　myself to feel, even, the first night air
on his naked chest, also the surprised
　　　　　first gasp when he dives and begins to drift,
numb and willing, out into the offing,
　　　　　stars taking over where the dusk caved in.

　　　What a gallon of water is when you
force yourself to drink it. Salt in the eye.
　　　　　The pressure of a fathom on the mind.
Should we applaud his helpless, flailing arms,
　　　　　disobedient to the very end?

Even the legs giving in, unfaithful
to the uneasy task of giving up.
    For those who love air and know how to swim,
we can only comprehend the knee-jerk
    impulse to stay afloat, the will to be

    upright, airtight. His body knew better,
we could say, and we could avoid what's next:
    there's the pistol he'll purchase in the morning
with just one bullet in it, and three wet
    drachmas he'll leave behind on the bar.

    There's that woman peeling onions who might hear,
and optimistic thistles by the road,
    and spatter on the eucalyptus tree,
and the verdict he knew we'd read into
    the last couplet of his abandoned shoes.

Thyrsus

That book was old as the corpse itself
and its tongue weight was too long a burden.
I said I'd read the ending if you asked,

the part about the satyr and the cliff.
We'd found a shady clearing on the beach
and had come to destroy ourselves with joy.

Smoke from some sacrifice stung our eyes
and pinecones were gathered at our feet
like loose grenades. In this kind of dream,

we knew they'd explode when they touched water.
Even the logic of the elements
had been sabotaged by our being there.

I offered to recite the middle instead,
showed you how the dry pages trembled
when I ransomed their sentences to air.

The book will know how to save us, I said,
and this wine in our glass is a mirror
we'll see through by reading in reverse.

No—start again at the beginning—
you said at last, then walked into the sea,
a pinecone balanced in your open palm.

Report from the Office of Optical Illusions

That noose draped over the oak's low branch:
    only a wasps' nest
      from which wasps have been evicted.
That glass of water you filled to the brim:
    an abandoned well
      drowning itself.
That ink spot the sun tattooed on your hand:
    only evidence
      of settlements on a desert map.
And that coin I placed on the railroad track:
    a key I left you
      so you'd open your box of bones.
And as for music through concrete walls:
    a song you once knew,
      some notes cut down with piano wire.
As for that body left bleeding on the pier:
    a rumpled corsage
      in the city's immaculate lapel.
And that blank page torn from the book:
    only a winding sheet
      upon which the dead refuse to write.
Those peaches softening in a blue bowl:
    just some accidents
      of ripeness.
Only fur and force, only awning and yawn,
    only press and particular,
      tangible throb.
And that bread and some salt from the sea:
    only bread and salt,
      only your bread, only my salt.

We stopped looking, for a few seconds,
     when you placed my hand
     on your real hip.
And my face, you also said,
     was like your face, my eyes
     just as blind, strange as anything.

Denial

We were hard at work with the starving,
a dozen white plates set out before us,
one copper coin in the middle of each.

We had learned to love what wasn't there,
our last milk left out for feral cats,
the barren pantry showing off its ribs.

Just yesterday, I'd braved the city's heart:
those avenues of squid and monkfish;
sweetbreads and steak displayed like relics

on their pillows of blood and melting ice.
Knowing I had resisted was enough
and I returned with unfilled paper bags

that you spent the afternoon unloading.
Here's the final pomegranate, you said,
making me gaze into an empty bowl.

Every night, in spite of such discipline,
hunger arrived an hour early, wanting
to collect on its debt. We didn't budge.

We bargained our coins, and even the plates,
mixed the rest of our flour with ashes
and let goats clean the bones of the garden.

In the end, all we had left was some air.
That would be our offering to the horse.
We hauled it out and waited at the wire,

but she pushed it away with her muzzle.
What she wanted was already here.
The grass she couldn't reach under our boots.

Translation

Bridge stones on your side of the river
are heavier than ours, your houses older.
Children born there have more excellent feet.

Some report crows blacker than our crows,
and censors less ruthless (but just as dumb).
Your caves, we know, make stinkier cheese.

Your dogs are rumored to be kinder,
your cats more insolent and beautiful.
Your telephone wires are musical staves.

Yet to say a woman rose to light a fire,
then went to gather wood in the forest,
explains neither the well nor the water.

And to say a man climbs a tower every day
to watch for smoke across the valley
tells us nothing new about desire.

I tried calling you an hour ago
to complain with my usual silence,
but calls are no longer going through.

Still, you waved to me from the other bank
when a blue rowboat passed under the bridge.
Both oars in conversation with the river.

Resistance

The sun had an agreement with the sea:
neither would move for at least an hour.

While I went deep, you waited on the boat,
watching for the anchor in the blue.

I'd made you come to the water at last.
Too many days we had been like statues,

numb objects in the garden with the bees.
Now gulls harassed the temple stones, circling

and dividing around us. From the shore,
old music from a world that had collapsed.

I broke the water's trance by dragging
a huge eel from its cave up to the boat.

My harpoon drummed the oarlocks as it flailed.
Then stillness, as it relaxed to molten jade.

17.xi.07

for Titos Patrikios

Drizzle all morning: the revolution
has to be postponed. Brave citizens
mob the streets, resume their Christmas shopping.

Wet taxis get lucky today
at Hotel Grande Bretagne. Now and then,
sunlight undresses the platitudes
of the Acropolis, pleasing all.

Where we retreat for our afternoon ouzo,
beside ruins of Hadrian's Library,
the jukebox won't take drachmas anymore;
but in the heaven of this *taverna*
students lie down with the generals,
relieving ancient sexual tensions.
Someone else's war spills its guts on TV.

As for me, well I'm Switzerland: alphorn,
yodel, and all, armed with forty wristwatches.
I can drink in any language.

Memory—always tactful, always sure—
will not open its umbrella in here.

Released from a book in my briefcase,
free once more to take his secret police
out for a stroll, even Ritsos
grumbles through the back door unnoticed.
He demands the last of my cigarettes,
ignores my jokes, scribbles inscrutable
faces on every cocktail napkin,
finishing each sentence the same one way:
the dead have no idea why they died.

Sentence

No one predicted we'd be sitting there,
just come in from a blizzard to that bar,
and three beached fishermen in the corner
would interrupt their beans to stare at us,
then return to eating, since we were strange
but cold enough to be left alone,
and that to expect their calm dismissal
of our being there showed we understood
how things worked then, in the dead decades,
after most of the city had vanished
on trains, or had been drowned in foreign ports;
and therefore, when the priest arrived
with his ice-crusted shawl and frozen cross,
crooning mangled hymns, his head gone to praise,
we'd think it right to offer him a seat,
would carry his stiff gloves to the fire,
and fill his glass with wine and pass him bread,
and would suffer the blessings he put
upon the empty wombs of our soup bowls;
and who knew we'd pretend to sing each verse
of the tune he'd use to condemn us,
but would have no answer to his slammed fist,
nor the thing he'd yell to be overheard
by everyone there—*when you stand this close*
to the other side, don't embarrass yourselves
with hope—as if that would be saying it all,
as if he knew we already stood there,
as if we could mount some kind of defense
before snow turned back to water in his beard.

Some Things along Strada C. A. Rosetti

Bucharest, April 2008

Far too quiet last night out on the street.
Dreams of police. Today we hog four chairs
in a café off Revolution Square,
where solitude and expensive coffee
agitate our collective memory.

The man in the blue bathrobe, he is ours,
blabbering, twisted like an ampersand
on his perch between bank and bar: one hand
on his cane, the other held out for beer.
He hasn't had a shave in nineteen years.

We claim the palaces and museums,
the royal portraits on the Atheneum,
but blame the stray dogs and immigrant scum
on the old regime, whose blank bravado
still hardens all the faces in the Metro.

This week the diplomats and presidents
will affirm Europe's doctrine in the East;
the yellow stars of the Union will increase
another star or two, new flags to cover
the old murals, the sickles and hammers.

Still, some things along Strada Rosetti
blur more than they clarify: budding trees
compete with wide Ottoman balconies
for the right to make shade. Light, meanwhile,
stagnates in a satellite dish. All style

is sacrificed to communication,
all music to the traffic's cloying hiss.
The beautiful civil servant knows this,
since she works with facts, and yet her high heels
and headphones imply there's something she feels

we all feel—we want to hear ourselves think,
we want to rise above the uniform
sidewalk blocks. The old cobblestones were torn
up years ago, along with the mansions
and monasteries. The old city was done

being old, we were informed. Not that we asked.
Those who were shot have had twenty years
to make peace with what they silenced here,
even if the dictator failed to confess.
His concrete horizon's left to remind us

what it takes to scare the mind out of a man.
We want to see ourselves too. The police
block every street today, but they're *our* police.
Neither gypsy dogs nor glue-sniffing teens
can take that from us. We know it means

something now to sit and read a book,
to read something true. Yes, we want to be
seen, but not to be watched—this, the relief
of a generation who couldn't say but knew
the National Library belonged to them too.

There are five real newspapers to read now
and a sign across the street can advertise
LEGAL TRANSLATIONS, but it's still not wise
to have speech handled by professionals.
Better now to just shut up, pay the bill,

join the amateur rabble on the street,
or claim a place along the balustrade.
Just outside, the uniformed riot squad
is shoring up its bulletproof phalanx.
The anarchists will refuse to break ranks,

will affirm their faith in all disorder.
Yes, we've had disorder. On this square,
in fact, here on display, the souvenir
of a body politic that has a soul:
our library, pocked with bullet holes.

Confession

Night came to hurt us from across the island,
resurrecting crickets in the old well.
You'd removed both of your arms and your hair
had turned to ash by the time I touched it.

If you go, I asked, how will we speak to those dead?
I said this knowing we couldn't ever.
Yet monks had put out a wooden table
and were waiting for the blood and bread.

All day, the mountain. Talking and falling apart.
I had to carry you most of the way.
All day: eternity and oranges,
stones and some fear I could and couldn't see.

Now, a half moon and the stars were roaring.
The orchard behind us was roaring too.
I couldn't bear their chanting anymore
and urged myself to disappear, like you.

Myth

On the stove, greens she stole from the mountain.
She gave an hour to pulling them apart.

Steam rose from the pot, pleasing the invisible.

He sat with his book by the back window,
reading the horizon for lightning:
stormy watches bringing the dark ship light.
Some ancient sentence broken on the page.

Outside, rain punished the earth for its crimes.
No, she said, the earth bore none of the guilt.
Proving it didn't care, a crow complained
to the cypress tree on behalf of all birds.

Three lemons on guard atop their blue plate.

Below the house, the sea surged into a cave.
No, she said again, the cave opened to the sea.

Possession, Macedonia

for EK, scribe

The swath of alphabet we scrawled in chalk
  smeared each time the seashell lurched
    and the dead lined up to have their say.

It would have been easier to write
  ourselves off as ceaseless grievers, Merrill-
    addicts, but when that dialogue began

with a detail only you knew, a thing
  out of old Armenia, kept secret
    by your family, we were completely swept

into the pit of blood we'd managed to dig.
  There are so many. Don't misunderstand,
    when the spirit (what else could we call her?)

named AHAG—a VICTIM OF THE MARCH—
  knocked at the mirror we propped so she'd
    SEE US through the glass, our game turned nightmare,

no going back. We gave three months to that table,
  exhausted, Lethe-drunk, while we scribbled
    down her uppercase appeals:

the story of her dying in the desert.
  Then she was gone. The voice that took her
    place spelled out FUCK YOU five times

before we wiped the surface clean, broke
　　　　every shell, slammed the heaviest door we could
　　　　　　　on the dead, then returned to living:

teaching classes in a stupor, going numb
　　　　with ouzo by four to keep the voices quiet.
　　　　　　　But they didn't wait more than a month

to come knocking again, no AHAG in sight.
　　　　I try not to remember it—that burning smell—
　　　　　　　how it got stronger the more we ignored it,

how it followed me as far as Olynthos.
　　　　Mares were grazing across the length of Thrace.
　　　　　　　In my dreams, they galloped beyond the last wells.

You said you dreamed of babies dipped in tar.
　　　　I waited, tended the fireplace while you slept.
　　　　　　　Outside, wind rattled the minarets of cypress.

If I remember anything, don't let it be
　　　　the wind they knocked from me one November
　　　　　　　at the old port, the night they took back

their voices, sharpening their teeth on my spine.
　　　　Three hours in Café Grotesque and my face
　　　　　　　changed shape, you told me later, as if hardened

for some invisible battleground.
    I scrawled on three cocktail napkins
        a contorted sketch of their ELSEWHERE

as dictated to me through an inch of cut crystal:
    two intersecting ovals and the ARROW TRAIL
        of our trajectory UP FROM THE DITCH.

Don't let it be the taste of wet cobblestone
    where they flung me, dragged by my scruff
        with a force I could only pin down after

as *pain*—my body brimming with it,
    splayed out by the stones of Agia Sophia
        where you kept me from leaping into traffic.

I remember two white cats gnawing squid
    by the pier. A red candle. Iconostasis.
        But they left nothing else I could salvage,

left me wading in salt up to my thighs
    while the barges fled to sea. Taste of brass,
        my own blood in my own mouth

where the bit hooked into my tongue.
      Four hours of disaster in your arms; a map
            I unlearned on the way back from there.

Then birdsong in the almond tree, slackened
      reins at first light—enough so I came back
            a ridden horse, ready to be broken.

Appeal

Every day, the island does its duty:
the cliff flaunting marble, because it can,
and salt water carousing with the sand.
Though bored with my circumspection, the sun
turns up on schedule, sets things on fire.

Source of this monotony, what do you require?
Same perfect shell, same body, same person.
The right weight of this beach stone in my hand.
Guilty of the crime of praise, here I am,
begging for an antidote to beauty.

Last Station of No One's Cross

Mount Athos

In an hour, nineteen needles
down from the fir. Ten blossoms

on the trunk of the Judas tree,
bruised beyond repair.

All morning, wreckage. As if
his own breath burned the blossoms.
The damage: him.

The cave is a mouth breathing him.
The earth is body, as it has to be
for pain to be so broad.

This cliff is its shattered hand.
Shelter, shatter. His soul won't scare.
He goes into his cave to pray.

I eat corpse, says a beetle going past.
I am corpse becoming corpse, he thinks,
though he thinks it too fast.

Lashed flesh won't bleed
enough for Heaven.

A bleached jawbone is such
beautiful Hell.

No bread or water. No novice
to fetch the bucket from its rope.

Through a fringe of tamarisk
he sees pollen
spun with dust in a blast from below,

the air he'd dangle in,
a rope round his waist. But to hang

too soon would filch what isn't his.
In a cell by the sea, last station

of no one's cross, counting
every needle as it falls.

No great guilt, but still a human face.
No relief from the agony of grace.

Still Life

With one brushstroke, it becomes spring.

Berries in a wooden bowl.

Some tulips, a limp sturgeon, a goblet of wine.
Roman bricks in the foundation of a church.
One leather glove still looking for a hand.

A surprise, that being born
we forget almost everything.

Security guards wait at the green gate
while sunlight over the wall
ignites their haloes of cigarette smoke.

Amphitheater

Being alone, the water seemed calmer,
his marble ledge more secure than it was.
There was one boat coming in, and music
from the *taverna* might have drawn him down.
Nothing but a few moments of rest,
some accounting of things tethered to him.
Beyond that only the mind, gone quiet.
Even the gulls forgot he was alive.

So it arrived, the beautiful sadness,
and he had to set a place for it:
a hollow sheared of everything but light.
Like that bare spot beneath the olive tree
lashed by the chain of a circling dog.

Exterior with Knife and Net

She said she sometimes saw their faces there,
    their profiles in slabs left by the sea.

Whole shelves sunk when the tide came,
    the smoother patches oiled with algae.

They followed bees down to a boulder
    tangled with a fisherman's red net.

She said it would never come loose.
    So he waded out with his knife

and cut a piece of it for her.
    I try to remember what they did next,

those people, if they took the long way back.
    Neither boulder nor sea giving way.

I think now of that wet net in her hands.

Kouros/Kore

1. Kouros

His marble skin had damaged light.

I woke the eyes with salt,
retrieved his scattered limbs,
returned to his torso the bowling ball head,
and fixed the fillet to hold his Delphic hair.

When he fell apart, I put back what I could.
So neither of us wasted our lives.

We remember horses and dogs we loved,
the flogged and the burned,
the bottomed-out chariots of Xerxes.
An isthmus we crossed, in opposite armies.
A thousand beards we might have grown.
Ten thousand dreams gone to seed.

As if we were one dreadlocked Doric column,
one archaic smile now revealing its sadness,
one spotlit shadow of something no longer there:
half god, half beast, one contemplative feast
fit for no king, fit for almost nothing.

And yet he stayed still long enough
so even I could shake my bones,
shed the rakish grin, the brain I'm in,
recast myself in his image of stone.

2. Kore

She moved a little when the wax inside
began to river. Wine gushed to the wing buds,

engorged the pomegranate she holds,
her two-ton wrist extended into space.

It takes centuries to admit some things:
the leather strap set loose upon her ankle,

currents of her chiton when she inhales,
the idea of Maria Callas on her tongue.

Had sing.
Now had been.

She's earned the rage of forty sybils.
Her mind's unfettered by symbols.

Those scars that decorate her arms
were made by the chisel or a blade?

He had to invent a new verb tense
to explain the stillness of those wings:

Had fly.
Now had rise.

Both present and past perfect,
entirely useless as speech.

With it, he counted his heresies
along the rosary of her spine.

3. Kouros

All night stone bled
and no light razed the shade.

I knew I'd find him buried at the end,

      his lost limbs marking
      the circumference of the field,

      every edge and chink of him silted
      till even he believed he couldn't move.

Somewhere overhead, petrified armies
blast their Sousa,
killing the last of my patience.

It's a mess to confess:
      I have steadied for forty years
      my bitter propositions,

      have driven my cart and plow
      over the bones of the dead:

      black strength
      strange blanks
      cracked rings

all voided by the things
workers unearthed this morning:

an earthquake rock,
a shadow clock,

and a tortoiseshell lyre
strung with catgut wires.

4. Kore

He should atone
for his long stay in dirty light
not seeing what's visible to her,

contours of a terrain
history never hooked fangs into:
groves of chickweed and nettle and clover
unmolested by ballads of the scythes.

Only obelisks of cypress trees.
Missing the exclamation points of graves.

The architecture of her brow was not
leveled by a bomb or Balkan wind
like some ordinary acropolis.
He should see what hasn't happened there.

He should correct
his lack of backsight, could rightly
hope to clear cliff when he jumps,
only the parachute of her peplos
there to save him, if she wants.

Never mind.
The darkness of sculpture limns its own line.
Even in bad museum light,
what's not there
about her
is what he loves.

And though her lips were marbled shut
he's heard her hum some hexachords.

He's also known what's brimming in her eyes:
that same water bore his weight
while he pitched last year, a leaky vessel,
the first cove west of Lendas, on Crete.

5. Kouros

He was hewn by a sledge
in the dreams of some tyrant Maecenas.

A crossbar to his skull,
chisel to his muzzle.

Even the cloves of his nipples chafe air.

I listened for years
to excavate the grit-clogged strain
caught in his throat,

a thing Mozart-glad,
merry as goat song,

variations on a pig Latin's kitsch.

Five times a day I stalked the plinth,
pillaging his unreasonable bliss,

a trail of syllables and half notes behind me,
his music I wanted to hamstring.

6. Kore

She burned shadows from his hiding place
    without ever moving her eyes

so all the big things went out with the small:

a barnacled shard, their dead dog's hair,
    and a gash the size of Alonissos.

She told him facts can always be mastered,
    the bullets and the bread and the keys,

harpoons, hecatombs, all filigree,
    letters burned in the voyage from below,

then brought him back in the wrong season,
    sped by wrong birds and backward winds,

sent him wheeling up the opposite coast
    without a sail attached to his mast,

sent air through what was left of his body.

She made him, in lashing rain,
                a hammer swung

at unsculpted marble,
            heart's shrapnel

shelves of sunken island breaking off.

7. Kouros

When he finally spoke
he split Naxian stone.

All his rifts
have seasoned this hillside.
No mob could tame
his asphodelic fields.

Has he peopled his shores?
Has he pebbled his minions?

Even bees remain biased
against the abstract certainties
of his face.

With how blank an eye
my stone beast stirs.

Two thousand summers
telling rain where to go,
letting no water in,
holding a worn flint fast.

He learned to outwit
a continent's meteorology.

Though coffin-legged now,
and awkward as a stone toad,
I know he'll rise
astride the mountain's spine,
take up the sagging reins,
and make this island walk again.

8. Kore

She says she hurts herself
becoming—
see the little raft-work of sea foam
adrift along the line left by the water?

Water's way of making light
of disappearance, she says.

Other signs left behind,
proving she's gone:
here the daggered traps of thornbush
where she dismounted the sea;

here some urns she filled
to nourish him.

Leave the usual
confusions to chance.
All the knowing's nothing
if the earth knows more of her.

If the sky's some lovely
glorious nothing,

and whether he believes or not,
and if that matters,

and if he flees

she hurts herself.

9. Kouros

Never more than a blunt plinth
a bleak plank, a blank.

Never too much rapture or repose:
never harpsichords,
nor gypsy oboes.

No more than some uncarved lines
where eyes could be,

black marble,
iron chisel at rest.

No peacocks,
no omnipotent feathers,
but headless columns, yes,
a charred garden.

Never an ornamental binge
or baroque tantrum

but mere sensation, yes,
a sound instrument:
one finger,
an invisible string,

and sometimes belief,
persistent as a weed.

10. Kore

To shroud her, she makes him take the loom,
knowing she'll undo everything he does.

> Five years of knots set loose,
> fibers gone off like ants into dust.

And though his kilim's off-kilter,
he's done his best to keep it glad:

> lozenges of wool made bright
> by boiling ox-eyed chamomile,

> and prescription bottle browns,
> and ground-beetle blacks,

> with a border of suicidal blue.

He watched her die daily.

Daily, she dyed my eyes.

> *Could we dissolve together,*
> *cadmium-cold?*

> *Turquoise tulip: my tantrum?*
> *Whorl of worsted green: my grace?*

His prayer rug of cochineal and lac.

Everything she didn't do
begged him to cut the thread.

11. Kouros

Strange planet, the head.

To admit a fissure or two,
a marble limb gone black and blue,
some orbiting round random suns:

all among expected outcomes.

> What he thinks about himself and sees
> means more than what he knows.
> I've studied his astrology,
> his braggadocio,
> and have only eclipsed his idiocy twice.

What he's taught me isn't nice.

Rather than speak,
he makes me sing:

Here's some sculpture, just some rock,
        nothing good to stall the clock;
any music of the spheres
        gathers forces, collapses here:

a block was cut, an arm broke off,
and standing tall or on his knees
all sculpted futures fall apart:
they're what the marble doesn't see.

12. Kore

However dull her once-red gown,
however cold her marble,
however failed the spindle's spin,
however black her olive,
however hard Mycenae burned,
however bright her pyres,
however rolled the stone away,
however barbed her wires,

however often she came home,
however smashed her clock,
however much she nearly died,
however much she lied,
however armies lost the war,
however her new borders,
however missing a whole year,
however she'd keep breathing,

however when the staircase broke,
however hard her landing,
however songs the children sang,
however rhyme was mangled,
however want, however marked,
however she'd keep breathing,
however wrong, he said, and her,
however she'd keep breathing.

13. Kouros

From a cave above Levadia
a gush of water turns a wheel
and there I remember at last:
      his statue once marked the place.

Here's where he was, Trophonius said,
ringed by sharpened logs,
so no one could touch,
so no one dare go down the pit.

Mobs cheered his departure with tear gas,
sacrificed three human girls
for no reason explained by the signs.

Deer still emerge at dusk, I've also learned,
to crop grass at cavern's edge.

Before the centuries brought me here,
he was gone,
ground to gravel to make a road,
a little lime for graves.

No inscription's hung around,
      no guide to show the way,
but anyway
      I took the rope to hang myself,

went willingly, please know,
in search of what I'd been,

and forgive me if I won't say
what I saw down there,
in the water's mirror.

Like all who went, I came back blind,
two stone almonds for my eyes:
no words forgotten in my rubble,
no peace remembered by my dead.

14. Kore

Yes, she was his labyrinth
and he climbed her ladder of cuts
      high as he could, dead ends at every turn,

never found his way, nor any middle to the bower,
if one was even there.

But he went to the locked gate and knocked
each hour for no answer,

knew beyond the brambled hedge
stone korai would be arranged:

      imperfect, ivy-wracked, allowed to be.
      Almost mortal, almost loved.

She let him stand, at least,
holding still as he could, and try,

      limited, yes, now that he was blind,
      but at the bottom of the cup

      he'd sometimes find another drop.
      That was plenty.

Cathedral, crown,
her plaited hair.

Her marble hands,
her absent stare.

Things they were. Things they are.

Yes—far as I could go—yes, far.

Altar

Maybe it's enough to say, in hindsight,
the conditions were right for bleeding there.

Maybe it's enough to know he swam at night,
climbed that jagged rock to offer the required flesh.

By then, he knew the dream had given all it had,
collapsing, as dreams do, into real seas.

The island took from him, then threw him
with a wave. And that was June.

Not by chance the blood turned back to water.
No accident that salt burned in the wound.

The idea of July was still too much.

Elegy

Your shoes were muddy from the graves,
so you left them out by the hitching post.

Those mornings before we vanished, like the horse.

That day's rain rinsed pollen from the air
and you said you could finally breathe.

Lilies were burning up there.
You held up three you'd cut for me to see,
then left them on the table when you went.

In a wooden box by the window, I hid
the black ribbon you used to tie your braid.
I couldn't bear to pick it up that day.
Something of your body still singed the air.

At night, you also burned: dreams of lilies,
horses, earth filling around us.
A centaur appeared in one, wearing my head.
I woke before it had a chance to speak.

Then today: a hoofprint outside the door
where you'd been walking. Or I had been.
It was hard to tell if we lived.

Either way, one of us had galloped back
after years of not being anywhere.
We had wanted so many years to be.
This piece of broken rope said that was true.

A Poem Not Written by Yannis Ritsos on the Day of My Birth

7/25/67

He arrived at the port too late,
threw his unused ticket to the ground.
Out on the jetty, a naked boy
stood pointing into the ship's wake,
where gulls knifed green water for squid.

He walked straight past the café,
didn't stop at the flower stall,
touch blue beads on the mule's harness,
or splash his face with fountain water.

On a list nailed to the butcher's red door,
he found his name, misspelled.
Do you see? another man asked,
pointing at the names that were crossed out.

Wasps strafed the eaves of the customs house
from their hangar of spit and newspaper,
and yet, early that morning, smoke had freed itself
from his ribbons of dusty tobacco.

Some meaning he found in three black plums,
a thimble of cold ouzo sipped at noon,
a blank canvas of stone in his pocket.

Confined by my white blanket,
I see none of this, of course,
since the lamps of my parents' house are off,
the shades drawn tight against midsummer,
the edicts of each shadow held at bay.

Squid Fishing

for Tasos Kouzis

When we wake the rowboat from its beach sleep
      it agrees to float, even surrenders
that fifth of island moonshine from the hull
      which we use to wash down our oranges.

There's a little chop that keeps us bobbing,
      helping us do what the squid require:
yank the lines hard every third breath or so.
      Let our jigged hooks romp along the bottom.

It's not like here down there. The beasts hover
      sideways, deeper than the light will go,
empty themselves out in order to move,
      follow bait up till they see our shadows.

Sometimes I'd take rain all afternoon
      and freezing hands, and sodden combat boots,
just to land one pitiful figure—
      like squid ejaculating salt water

say, which has some psychological truth
      at the level of obvious symbol,
or, *like squid coughing clouds of homemade ink,*
      if I needed to show my jealousy;

or, *these squid barking air in a bucket,*
      if misery was what I translated.
There's some satisfying truth beyond all this:
      the grill, some lemon, the new olive oil.

As if we could really go out fishing
        to empty such ideas from ourselves.
Poor words, swimming for shore from a rowboat.
        Half the time my line was tangled on the oar.

But the cove has already said enough.
        The marble cliffs conduct light until dusk.
The squid invent new colors as they die.
        These offerings of orange peel for its depths.

The Skyros Papers

Arriving there isn't what you're destined for . . .

1

I'd have liked my arrival more without the wind.
      Everything here is exhausted by it.
It howls across scrub hills with explosions of grit.
      Tonight it scatters all my scratch paper,
old photocopies of Cavafy's "Ithaka,"
      in fact, all painfully blank on one side.
      I save only six, stopped by a rock wall.

2

My first full day of emptiness, which I squander
      in conversation with Kyria E——.
She says the wind *can churn the mind* and leave one mad.
      I might prefer that. No words came today.
I wanted at least to name the purple blossoms
      Kyria left in a vase by my door.
      But I was speechless before their wilting.

3

My feet soak in a clay bowl painted with green fish:
      some swimming south, the others north. I try
to hold myself still. Nothing else here has to try,
      not the birds, nor the neighbor's pregnant cat,
not my collection of shells and polished driftwood.
      They move, or are still. And olive leaves sing
      when gusts sent by the headland quicken them.

4

To escape the air, I spend days underwater,
       a loaded spear gun ready in my hand.
But each time I dive, I find a seafloor littered
       with plastic: tarps, bleach bottles, fishing line,
and thirty feet deep off Pefka, a whole white chair.
       No Ithaka at all. What Skyros gave
       was garbage, not the joy of new harbors.

5

But something broke beside the grave of Rupert Brooke,
       who died here, *corner of a foreign field.*
And while the love of country's not so strong in me,
       I leave the place stirred, return home to find
the pregnant cat curled up in my foot bowl, purring.
       One page left. I could mark it tomorrow.
       The green fish alive, swimming circles now.

6

Kyria E——brings me apricots this morning,
       my last on Skyros, so I kiss her twice.
When I ask, she calls the blossoms *paschalitsa,*
       blooming thanks to the same wind that wrecks them.
But nothing can hold summer back, at least not long.
       I leave that afternoon, writing only:
       The place has wind. It has blown clear through me.

Troppo Mare

You already tried to drown me three times.
　　　　Yucatan. Thasos. Crete.

And I admit I deserve your violence.
　　　　Too much doubt. Too much surface weight.

But I resent you even more tonight
　　　　for what you did, just now, before dark:

such redundant perfection, going beyond blue
　　　　to blood-purple past the escarpment,

spilling me and the whole island off your ledge.
　　　　I've had too much of abundance.

I've had too much of you, sea.
　　　　Too much of your clarity. Too much depth.

Still, I steady myself from this height
　　　　for another dive, stubborn as that crab

whose torn leg you carved out with your tongue.
　　　　I rescued it from the bottom this morning,

a lock of sea grass still tangled in the claw.
　　　　I have clung like that, watching my fingers slip.

Take every hollow carapace and shattered limb,
 grind it all to nothing, along with me.

Before then, let me surface just once more.
 I ask, in the holy name of what is less.

Stake

After sex, we went out to find our eyes
in the dusty wells of espresso cups.
You produced at least two good ideas
we weren't able to pursue
when the man with the cello threw us off
the jagged cliffs of his Donizetti.
Even the bottles of water shut up.

In that light a sparrow worked our crumbs.
Some planets moved.
Three punks rolled joints beneath Bruno,
whose memory refused to burn.

At five, someone came selling lodestones.
Beautiful waitresses plied the cops with booze.
Priests wept in their prosecco.

And all the while, children with bare feet
kicked the lost head of a statue,
cheering each time they scored a goal.

We knew that even in Rome,
here in the Campo de' Fiori,
where everyone came or left with a bouquet,
where the shadows, we hardly believed,
had turned into wine,
we shouldn't keep our secrets to ourselves.

Recessional

Aqueduct, *hamam*, and broken wall.
Stray dogs and people on leashes.

The same repeated hour for twenty years:
on the third step
of the city's thirtieth church,
a boy scrawls a name
with the sharp edge of a stone.

He hears the liturgy chanted by pigeons,
sees missing water, the unclean
clean again, the wall restored
with battlements for Roman soldiers.

If he climbed to the roof of the building
across the street, he might even see himself.

Every afternoon a brief shower.
Then an hour of sun, when the city
comes out to pace along the port.

Then another boy, or the same one,
rises from sleep in a cramped room,
opens curtains to let light in,
and goes out to kiss the icons,
light candles for one not long dead.

Defiance

Another body found in the harbor,
you told me, but they could not bring it up.

Your hair was dripping and your lips were blue.
When you lifted the tea cup, your hands shook.

Tell me, I said.
But you were hiding behind the cold,

staring deep into the cup
where no questions were going to reach you.

Rain drummed the window and the room
smelled of sulfur and candle wax.

Your gaze was fixed (it happened that way
with you sometimes) so there was nothing

to do but wait. I'd covered your photograph
with a black scarf, and had taken

down all the mirrors as you'd asked,
left them facing the wall in the other room.

Tell me what you see in there, I said.
You said you couldn't see, now that you were dead.

Thing is, we almost had it. I knew, since I
was there too. First the heel,

then her whole foot emerged, still attached
to its bronze leg. Sardines were in that net too,

throwing themselves over the bridge
of her calf into air.

I'd just glimpsed where water burned the skin
on her back to green. Then the rope snapped.

But look, I said, in case you'd listen,
your boots are still here by the door, leaking water.

Interior with a Bowl of Matches

Because something's missing from the room,
he goes out.
It's beside the millstone in the garden.

Because the cliff rises behind the house,
she comes naked from the bath,
puts a red blanket on the bed and doesn't sleep.

A moth tastes light caught in the mirror.
A broken cork, wine.
The window, rain.

Because it is September,
he returns hungry.

The ceiling's wooden beams don't hold.
Nails pry loose from the floorboards.

A shallow bowl of wooden matches
trembles on the cabinet by the door.
And a vase with one drenched poppy.

Outside, the sea, indifferent as glass.

Notes

"Impressions of a Drowning Man": The Greek poet Kostas Karyotakis failed to drown himself on July 20, 1928. He shot himself in Preveza the following day. The excerpts from his suicide note were translated by William W. Reader and Keith Taylor.

"17.ix.07": November 17 is Polytechnic Day in Greece, celebrating the 1973 student-led revolt against the military junta; "the dead have no idea why they died," Yannis Ritsos, "The Second Coming" (translated by Edmund Keeley and Phillip Sherrard).

"Some Things along Strada C. A. Rosetti": The Romanian National Library sits in the heart of Bucharest on what used to be Piața Palatului. The square was renamed Piața Revoluției in 1989, since it was here that the Romanian Revolution began in earnest, culminating in the death of Nicolae Ceaușescu that December. In 2008 Romania (a new member of the European Union) hosted the twentieth annual NATO summit in Bucharest. Strada C. A. Rossetti is named for the writer and politician Constantin Alexandru Rosetti, who descended from Phariot Greeks and who took part in the Wallachian Revolution of 1848.

"Myth": "stormy watches bringing the dark ship light," Alcaeus, "Hymns" (translated by M. L. West).

"Last Station of No One's Cross": Matthew 6:6.

"Kouros/Kore": Both "kouros" and "kore" indicate archetypes of Greek sculpture—of a young man and of a young woman. Section 3, "Drive your cart and plow over the bones of the dead," William Blake,

Proverbs of Hell. Section 8, "You fill up the urns here and nourish the heart," Paul Celan, "Sand from the Urns." (translated by Michael Hamburger); "Still when, to where thou wert, I came, / Some lovely glorious nothing I did see . . . ," John Donne, "Aire and Angels."

"A Poem not Written by Yannis Ritsos on the Day of My Birth": In 1967 Ritsos was arrested and forbidden to publish under the military dictatorship of Colonel Yiorgos Papadopoulos.

"The Skyros Papers": "Arriving there isn't what you're destined for," C. P. Cavafy, "Ithaka" (translated by Edmund Keeley and Phillip Sherrard); ". . . corner of a foreign field," Rupert Brooke, "The Soldier."

"Troppo Mare": "Troppo mare. Ne abbiamo veduto abbastanza di mare," Cesare Pavese, "Gente Spaesata."